Therapeutic Massages for Pets: Strengthening the Special Bond

Author: Gonzalo Estrada

While every precaution has been taken in the preparation of this book, the publisher assumes no responsibility for errors or omissions, or for damages resulting from the use of the information contained herein.

THERAPEUTIC MASSAGES FOR PETS

First edition. March 13, 2024.

ISBN: 979-8224539741

Written by Gonzalo Estrada.

Table of Contents

Content.

Chapter 1: The importance of therapeutic massage for pets

Learn how therapeutic massage can strengthen the special bond with your pet and improve their overall well-being.

Introduction

In the world of pets, the emotional bonds we share with our faithful companions are truly special. Whether you have a dog or a cat, a bird or a guinea pig, our pets provide us with unconditional love and unparalleled companionship. However, did you know that therapeutic massage can further enhance this connection and improve your overall well-being? In this chapter, we'll explore the importance of therapeutic massage for pets, and how this practice can strengthen the bond you share with your beloved furry friend.

The ancient art of therapeutic massage

Therapeutic massage for pets has its roots in ancient care and healing practices used in different cultures around the world. From traditional Chinese medicine to indigenous cultures in Latin America, massage has been used for centuries to promote physical and emotional health and well-being.

In the case of pets, therapeutic massage has become an increasingly popular technique recognized for its effectiveness in maintaining health and preventing diseases. Through physical contact, gentle caresses and specific movements, massage therapists work on the muscles and tissues of pets, releasing accumulated tension and stimulating blood flow.

Benefits of therapeutic massage for pets

The benefits of therapeutic massage for pets are extraordinary. It not only promotes better blood circulation and relieves muscle tension, but it also contributes to a better functioning of the lymphatic system and strengthens the immune system. In addition, therapeutic massage can help relieve joint pain and improve mobility in older pets or pets with chronic medical conditions.

But did you know that massage can also have a significant impact on your pet's emotional well-being? Just like us, animals can experience stress, anxiety, and depression. Therapeutic massage releases endorphins and promotes a sense of calm and relaxation in animals, helping them to reduce these negative emotional states. In addition, by strengthening the special bond you have with your pet, therapeutic massage promotes greater trust and security.

Strengthening the special bond with your pet through therapeutic massage

Therapeutic massage is an opportunity to connect on a deeper level with your pet. By dedicating time and energy to giving your furry friend a massage, you're showing your love and concern for their well-being. This practice strengthens the emotional bond, creates an environment of trust and mutual respect, and improves communication between the two.

When you get ready to massage your pet, be sure to create a peaceful environment free of distractions. Remember that every pet is unique, so it's important to observe their reactions and adapt the massage to their specific needs. Start with gentle, slow movements, applying appropriate pressure to your body. Listen to your pet and see how it responds to each caress.

Unfinished conclusions

Therapeutic massage offers a world of possibilities to strengthen your pet's overall well-being and reinforce the special bond they share. Through the therapeutic massage technique, you can provide your furry friend with physical and emotional relief, and improve their quality of life. But this is just the beginning of our journey through pet massage, as there's still so much more to discover and explore. Join us in the second half of this chapter, where we will delve into the techniques and tips for performing an effective therapeutic massage. You don't want to miss what comes next! Additional Benefits of Therapeutic Massage for Pets

In addition to the impressive physical and emotional benefits offered by therapeutic massages to our pets, there are other outstanding advantages worth mentioning. As we delve deeper into this ancient practice, we discover a myriad of gains that can contribute to improving the quality of life of our beloved furry companion.

One of the most outstanding benefits of therapeutic massage is its ability to strengthen the digestive system of our pets. Gentle and properly applied abdominal massage can help stimulate digestion and prevent gastrointestinal problems such as gas accumulation and constipation. By promoting a better functioning of the digestive system, therapeutic massage contributes to an adequate absorption of nutrients and the elimination of toxins, which translates into better overall health for our pet.

In addition, therapeutic massage can help relieve stress caused by changes in the environment or traumatic events, such as visits to the vet or moving. Through specific massage techniques, we can help calm and relax our pets, providing them with a haven of well-being during stressful times. This can also be especially beneficial for animals that have experienced trauma or abuse in the past, as therapeutic massage can help them to regain trust in human beings and to overcome difficult situations.

Another surprising benefit of therapeutic massage is its ability to strengthen the muscular and bone systems of our pets. By working muscles and tissues through specific movements, we help to tone our muscles and improve the mobility of our pets. This is especially important in older animals or in those that suffer from joint conditions, such as arthritis. Therapeutic massage can help relieve pain, reduce inflammation and improve joint function, resulting in a better quality of life for our beloved pets.

In addition, therapeutic massage can serve as a tool for the early detection of possible health problems in our pets. During the massage, we can detect physical abnormalities such as lumps, excessive sensitivity, or changes in skin texture. By being in tune with our pet's body, we can notice any changes that may require medical attention and thus seek the right treatment as soon as possible.

Conclusion

Therapeutic massage is a powerful and versatile practice that can strengthen the special connection we have with our pets and improve their overall well-being. From relieving muscle aches and improving circulation to easing stress and strengthening the digestive system, the benefits of therapeutic massage are countless.

As pet owners, it's our duty to provide them with love, care, and constant attention. Therapeutic massage offers us the opportunity to connect on a deeper level with our pets, strengthening our relationship and creating an environment of mutual trust. By dedicating time and energy to providing them with this treatment, we are making a significant contribution to their physical and emotional well-being.

In the second half of this chapter, we'll explore techniques and practical tips for performing effective therapeutic massage on our pets. You don't want to miss out on this invaluable information that will help you provide your furry friend with a safe, pleasant and beneficial therapeutic massage experience. Keep reading and discover everything you need to know to become an expert in therapeutic massages for pets!

Chapter 2: The Physical Benefits of Massage for Pets

Learn about the physical benefits that therapeutic massage can provide to your pet, from muscle relaxation to improved circulation.

Therapeutic massage is an ancient practice that has been used to alleviate ailments and promote healing in human beings. But did you know that it can also be beneficial for your beloved pets? Therapeutic massages can not only help keep your furry companion relaxed and calm, but they can also boost their physical well-being.

One of the most notable benefits of therapeutic massage for pets is the muscle relaxation it provides. Like humans, animals can also suffer from muscle tension and stiffness, especially those who lead an active lifestyle or suffer from medical conditions. Through gentle movements and appropriate techniques, therapeutic massage can help release the tension built up in your pet's muscles, thus promoting greater flexibility and mobility.

In addition to relaxing muscles, therapeutic massage also stimulates your pet's blood circulation. This means that the flow of oxygenated blood to tissues and organs is increased, which in turn promotes better function of these vital systems. Improved circulation can be especially beneficial for older pets, as it promotes cell regeneration and can alleviate discomfort related to arthritis or inflammatory conditions.

Another physical benefit of massage for pets is its ability to stimulate the lymphatic system. The lymphatic system is responsible for eliminating toxins and other wastes from the body, thus strengthening the immune system. Through gentle movements and lymphatic drainage techniques, therapeutic massage can help your pet eliminate accumulated toxins and improve their overall health.

Therapeutic massage can also have a positive impact on your pet's nervous system. Studies have shown that gentle, conscious physical contact, such as that provided during a massage, can release endorphins and reduce levels of stress and anxiety. This is especially relevant for pets that have experienced trauma or are suffering from behavioral problems. By helping your pet to relax and release emotional tension, therapeutic massage will further strengthen your special bond and promote their overall well-being.

These are just a few examples of the physical benefits that therapeutic massage can provide to your pet. As a responsible owner, you can learn to apply proper and safe massage techniques to ensure that your partner gets the most out of this experience. However, it is important to remember that therapeutic massage should not replace professional medical treatment in the event of illness or injury. Always consult your veterinarian before starting any complementary therapy for your pet.

In the second half of this chapter, we'll explore other physical benefits of massage for pets, as well as techniques and practical tips for performing therapeutic massages at home. Discover how to strengthen your pet's physical well-being through the healing power of massage! Keep reading in the next chapter. Therapeutic massage can provide your pet with a number of physical benefits, as we explored in the first half of this chapter. But that's not all, there's still more to discover about how this ancient practice can strengthen your furry companion's physical well-being. Let's continue to explore other benefits and techniques of therapeutic massage that can help improve your pet's quality of life.

In addition to relaxing muscles and improving circulation, therapeutic massage can help relieve pain in pets. If your animal is suffering from chronic pain due to an injury or illness, such as arthritis, therapeutic massage can be a natural and safe way to provide relief. Through gentle movements and appropriate techniques, you can work on specific areas of your pet's body that need attention and relieve muscle tension. This can reduce inflammation and promote greater mobility, which in turn can improve your furry friend's quality of life.

Another physical benefit of therapeutic massage for pets is the improvement of the respiratory system. By using deep breathing techniques during the massage, you can help your pet breathe more efficiently and better oxygenate the tissues. This can be especially beneficial for those pets that suffer from respiratory diseases, such as asthma. In addition, therapeutic massage can help relieve chest congestion and facilitate better breathing.

We can't forget to mention the benefits of therapeutic massage on your pet's digestive system. Abdominal massage can stimulate proper digestive system function, promoting better absorption of nutrients and elimination of waste. If your pet is suffering from digestive problems, such as constipation or indigestion, therapeutic massage can be a useful addition to your treatment plan. Be sure to use gentle, circular clockwise techniques to effectively stimulate the gastrointestinal tract.

In addition to all these physical benefits, therapeutic massage can also have positive effects on your pet's emotional well-being. As we mentioned earlier, gentle, conscious physical contact during massage can release endorphins and reduce levels of stress and anxiety. This is especially important for pets that have experienced trauma or are suffering from behavioral problems. By helping your pet to relax and release emotional tension, therapeutic massage can further strengthen your special bond and promote their overall well-being.

To safely and effectively apply therapeutic massage to your pet, it's important to consider certain aspects. First, you need to make sure that both you and your pet are in a relaxed and calm environment, free of distractions. It's also essential to understand your pet's limits and preferences. Some animals may not enjoy certain types of touches or movements, so it's important to watch their body language and adjust the technique accordingly.

Always remember that therapeutic massage should not replace professional medical treatment in case of illness or injury. If your pet is experiencing any health problems, it's important to check with your veterinarian before starting any complementary therapy.

In conclusion, therapeutic massage can provide a wide range of physical benefits to your pet, from muscle relaxation to pain relief and improvement of the respiratory and digestive system. This ancient practice can strengthen both the physical and emotional well-being of your furry companion, and as long as you follow the right techniques and consult your veterinarian, you can provide your pet with a pleasant and beneficial experience. Continue to explore and learn about the healing power of massage therapy in caring for your pets.

Chapter 3: The Emotional Benefits of Massage for Pets

Explore how therapeutic massage can help calm anxiety, reduce stress and improve your pet's mood.

In everyday life, just like us, pets also experience different emotions and moods. Whether they are facing a stressful situation, such as a visit to the vet or a severe storm, or simply need to relax after a busy day, therapeutic massage can be a wonderful tool to help them feel better emotionally.

Stress and anxiety are common problems for pets, especially when they are in new or unfamiliar situations. Fortunately, therapeutic massage can be an effective solution to combat these emotional problems. By providing a calm and relaxed environment, as well as gentle and comforting massage techniques, pet owners can help their loyal companions find comfort and relief.

One of the main emotional benefits of massage for pets is the ability to calm anxiety. By using gentle, rhythmic movements, therapeutic massage can help lower stress and anxiety levels in animals. This is because massage activates the body's relaxation response, stimulating the release of endorphins, also known as the hormones of happiness. These endorphins help to induce a state of calm and well-being in the pet, which in turn reduces anxiety symptoms.

In addition to calming anxiety, therapeutic massage can also reduce stress in pets. Many times, animals can experience stress due to situations that they consider threatening or triggering. By providing a safe and comforting environment, massage can help reduce muscle tension and release accumulated energy, allowing stress to dissipate. This way, pets can find relief and an overall sense of peace of mind.

The mood of our pets can also greatly benefit from therapeutic massage. Just like in humans, massage can help to release endorphins in animals, thus improving their overall mood. Studies have shown that animals that receive regular massages tend to be happier and less likely to develop behavioral problems related to stress and anxiety. By maintaining a positive mood, our pets can enjoy a fuller and healthier life.

Therapeutic massage not only provides emotional benefits to our pets, but it also strengthens the special bond we share with them. Through loving touch and positive interactions during the massage, we can establish and strengthen trust and communication with our furry friends. This time dedicated to the well-being of our pets strengthens the relationship and creates a deeper bond between the owner and the pet.

The first half of this chapter has explored how therapeutic massage can calm anxiety, reduce stress and improve the mood of pets. Now that we have established the emotional benefits of this practice, in the second half of this chapter we will focus on learning the specific massage techniques that we can use to provide our pets with these benefits. These techniques will allow you to take care of your beloved pet in an even more special and meaningful way. Are you ready to discover everything you can do to give your furry companion a unique therapeutic massage experience? Keep reading in the second part of this chapter. The specific massage techniques you can use to provide your pets with the emotional benefits of therapeutic massage are simple but effective. With a little practice and patience, you can become an expert in massages for your furry companion.

One of the most common techniques is rubbing massage. This technique involves using circular, gentle movements to gently scrub your pet's body. Start by stroking your neck and shoulders, then move to your back and finally to your hind legs. Pay attention to areas where your pet is showing tension or stiffness and apply a little more pressure to those points. Remember to always keep a steady pace and show your pet that you are relaxed and calm during the massage.

Another technique you can use is kneading massage. This technique involves gently pressing and releasing your pet's muscles with your fingers and hands. Start at the neck and, using your thumbs, gently press the muscles in a circular motion. You can then move to your shoulders, back and hind legs, paying special attention to any area where your pet has knots or muscle tension. This type of massage can be especially beneficial for pets that tend to have tight or stiff muscles.

In addition to the rubbing and kneading massage, you can also use the gentle pressure technique to help relieve stress and anxiety in your pet. This technique involves applying pressure to specific points on your pet's body using your fingers or the palms of your hands. Start by applying gentle pressure to the base of your pet's spine and then move to the shoulders and hind legs. As you apply pressure, stay calm and watch your pet's reactions. Some pets may enjoy stronger pressure, while others prefer softer pressure, so adjust the intensity according to your pet's needs.

Always remember to consider your pet's comfort during the massage. If at any time your pet shows signs of discomfort or discomfort, stop the massage and give it some time to relax. It's important to respect your pet's limits and adapt massage techniques to their individual needs.

As you become more familiar with these massage techniques, you can adapt and combine them according to what works best for your pet. There is no single, right approach, as every pet is unique and may have specific preferences. The most important thing is that the massage is a positive and relaxing experience for your feline or canine companion.

Over time, you'll not only see the emotional benefits of massage for your pet, but you'll also strengthen that special and unique bond you have with them. Therapeutic massage is an opportunity to connect with your pet on a deeper level, showing love and care through the comforting power of touch.

Keep exploring and learning new massage techniques, and enjoy this quality time with your pet. Therapeutic massage will not only improve your pet's emotional health, but it will also strengthen the relationship you share, making both of you feel happier and more connected.

So don't wait any longer, start experimenting with these massage techniques and discover the incredible healing power they have in your pet. I assure you that your furry companion will thank you with thankful licks and purrs!

Chapter 4: Getting Ready to Massage Your Pet

Learn the basic techniques and elements necessary to give your pet therapeutic massages in the comfort of your home.

Giving your pet therapeutic massages can be a wonderful experience for both them and you. Not only will you strengthen the special bond you share with your faithful companion, but you'll also provide physical and emotional benefits to your pet. What could be better than helping to ease your tensions and promote your overall well-being? In this chapter, we'll learn the basic techniques and key elements necessary for you to begin giving your pet therapeutic massages.

Before starting massages, it's important to create a relaxed and peaceful environment. Choose a comfortable place in your home where both you and your pet feel at ease. Make sure the room is at a comfortable temperature and turn off any sources of noise or distraction. The right environment is crucial for you to enjoy a pleasant and effective massage session!

Now, let's talk about the elements necessary to give your pet therapeutic massages. First of all, make sure you have a massage oil or cream suitable for animals on hand. These products are designed especially for your pet's sensitive skin and help reduce friction during massage. You can find them in specialty pet stores or check with your trusted veterinarian for recommendations.

In addition to the oil or cream, you'll need a soft, padded surface where your pet can comfortably relax. You can use a soft blanket or a special pet mat. Make sure it's big enough for your pet to stretch and move freely.

Now that you have all the necessary items, it's time to learn the basic techniques of therapeutic massage for your pet. Remember that it's vital to consider your pet's size and physical condition, as well as their tolerance to touch and pressure.

Start with soft, gentle movements, gently stroking your pet's coat. This helps to relax you and prepare you for the massage. See how your pet responds and adjust the intensity and pressure according to their needs. Some pets may be more sensitive than others, so be aware of any signs of discomfort and modify your technique accordingly.

As you become more comfortable, you can explore different massage techniques, such as kneading and friction. These techniques help to release tension and promote better blood circulation. Always remember to work towards the growth of your pet's coat and pay attention to all areas of the body, including the neck, back, legs and abdomen.

It's important to remember that therapeutic massage for pets is not a substitute for professional veterinary care. Always check with your veterinarian before starting any massage program, especially if your pet has a pre-existing medical condition or has experienced recent injuries.

So, now you have the basic knowledge and the necessary elements to start giving therapeutic massages to your pet. Get ready to embark on an incredible adventure of well-being and connection with your faithful companion! Continue reading our next chapter and discover advanced therapeutic massage techniques that will make your pet feel even better. Don't miss it!

In the second half of this chapter, I'll teach you some additional tips so you can maximize the benefits of therapeutic massages for your pet.

One of the keys to giving a good therapeutic massage is to establish an emotional connection with your pet. Before you begin, take a few minutes to caress and talk softly to him. This will help create a relaxed environment and allow your pet to feel safe and comfortable next to you.

During the massage, pay attention to your pet's cues. Observe their body language and how they react to different movements and techniques. If you notice that your pet is showing signs of tension or discomfort, adjust the pressure or switch to a milder technique.

Remember that every pet is unique and will have individual preferences when it comes to massages. Some may enjoy a more energetic massage, while others will prefer softer and more delicate movements. Explore different techniques and, over time, you'll get to know what's best for your furry companion.

Another important aspect to consider is the duration of the massages. Just like humans, pets can have different levels of tolerance to massage. Start with short sessions of about five minutes and see how your pet reacts. If it seems comfortable, you can gradually increase the length of your sessions. However, it's important not to exceed the recommended time, as this can cause fatigue or stress for your pet.

As you become more confident in your massage skills, you can begin to use more advanced techniques. For example, gentle stretching can be beneficial in relieving muscle stiffness and increasing your pet's flexibility. Always remember to do it carefully and gently, avoiding sudden movements, especially if your pet has a pre-existing medical condition.

In addition, it's important to pay attention to your pet's problem areas. If you notice that your pet has a specific area of tension or sensitivity, dedicate more time and attention to that area during the massage. You can apply softer, more circular movements to help relax and relieve discomfort.

Finally, it's essential that both you and your pet enjoy the process. Therapeutic massages are an opportunity to strengthen the special bond you share with your pet while providing physical and emotional benefits. Take advantage of this time to connect with your pet, transmitting love and well-being through your hands and your calm presence.

Remember that it is always recommended to consult your veterinarian before starting any therapeutic massage program for your pet. They can provide you with additional guidance and ensure that massages are safe and beneficial for your furry friend.

Congratulations on getting here on your way to learn how to give your pet therapeutic massages! Now you're ready to apply what you've learned and provide your pet with moments of relaxation and well-being. Continue to enjoy this wonderful experience and continue to connect with your faithful companion through therapeutic massages. Your pet will thank you!

Chapter 5: The Language of Touch

Learn how to read your pet's signals and adapt the therapeutic massage to their needs and preferences.

Therapeutic massage is an ancient technique that has been used to promote relaxation, relieve stress and improve health in both humans and animals. For our beloved pets, therapeutic massage is an extraordinary tool to strengthen the special bond we share with them.

Unlike human beings, our pets cannot verbally communicate with us to express their needs and preferences. However, their bodies speak their own language, and through touch we can learn to interpret and respond to the signals they give us. Every touch, every caress, is an opportunity to connect with our furry companions and understand their desires and emotional states.

It's essential to remember that every pet is unique, with its own personality and experiences. Some animals may enjoy physical contact and will constantly seek our caresses, while others may be more reserved and require a more subtle and respectful approach. Carefully observing our pet's reactions during the massage will allow us to know their individual preferences and adapt our technique to provide them with the most pleasant experience.

One of the keys to understanding the language of touch in our pets is to pay attention to their body language. As responsible owners, we must learn to read the signs shown by their posture, facial expression and movements in order to adapt the massage to their specific needs.

For example, if we notice that our pet relaxes, closes its eyes and its muscles loosen when receiving the massage, we are on the right track. Conversely, if you show signs of discomfort or tension, we should adjust our technique or stop if necessary.

In addition to posture and facial expression, breathing rate is another important indicator of the well-being of our pets during the massage. A slow, deep breathing rate usually indicates relaxation and satisfaction. When our pets enjoy the massage, their breathing becomes more regular and calm. Conversely, restless or shortness of breath can be a sign of tension or discomfort. Being aware of these subtle changes in breathing will help us adjust our technique and ensure that we provide the right massage for our pets' well-being.

Each pet also has specific areas on their body that may be more sensitive or prone to tension. Some dogs, for example, may especially enjoy a massage at the base of their tails, while others love to be stroked behind their ears. Cats, on the other hand, may prefer massages on the neck and spine area. Paying attention to the reactions and preferences of our pets will allow us to reach a deeper level of connection and mutual satisfaction during therapeutic massage.

In short, learning the language of touch in our pets is a valuable tool to strengthen our special bond and provide them with the care they deserve. Through the observation and adaptation of our technique, we can discover how to read the signals that our pets give us during the massage and provide them with an experience of optimal relaxation and well-being. Now, dive into the world of therapeutic massage for pets and discover the power of touch in our shared lives.

Therapeutic massage is an invaluable tool for strengthening the special bond we share with our pets. Through touch, we can communicate with them in a unique and profound way. In the first half of this chapter, we have learned to read the signals that our pets send us during the massage, adapting our technique to meet their individual needs and preferences.

Continuing our exploration of the language of touch, it's also important that we pay attention to how our pets respond to different types of pressure and movement during the massage. Some animals may prefer gentle, gentle caresses, while others may enjoy a firmer, more energetic massage. It is essential to find the right balance and adjust our technique according to the preferences of our pets.

In addition, we must be aware of how therapeutic massage affects the emotional state of our pets. Just as we experience a sense of relaxation and well-being after a massage, our pets can also experience an increase in their mood and a decrease in stress levels. Observing how their facial expressions, movements and general attitude change during and after the massage will give us an idea of how they feel.

Our pets may also tell us what areas of their body they prefer for us to focus on during the massage. Some dogs may especially enjoy a massage on their hind legs, while others may like petting their necks. Cats, on the other hand, may show a preference for a massage of the head or in the area of the spine. Being attentive to these signs will allow us to provide them with a more pleasant and beneficial massage.

As we move forward in our therapeutic massage practice for pets, it's key to remember that each animal is unique and may have different reactions and preferences. What works for one dog may not work for another, and vice versa. It is necessary to be patient and flexible, adapting our technique to meet the individual needs of our pets.

In addition to the massage itself, it is also important to create a relaxing and safe environment for our pets during the massage session. This includes eliminating any distractions or interferences, such as loud noises or unwanted visitors. A quiet and peaceful space will allow our pets to relax and fully surrender to the massage experience.

Finally, therapeutic massage for pets should not be an isolated activity, but an integral part of our relationship with them. Regular massages provide us with an opportunity to deeply connect with our pets, further strengthening our special bond. In addition, therapeutic massage can be beneficial to your overall health and well-being, helping to relieve aches and pains, improve blood circulation and promote relaxation.

In short, the language of touch allows us to communicate with our pets in a unique and meaningful way. Through observation and adaptation of our technique, we can learn to read the signals they give us and provide them with a therapeutic massage that meets their individual needs. In doing so, we strengthen our special bond and provide them with the care and attention they deserve.

Continue to explore the power of therapeutic massage for pets and discover the beauty of this enriching practice. Our furry companions are waiting for us with open arms (or legs), ready to enjoy an experience of relaxation and well-being with us.

Chapter 6: Massages to Relieve Stress and Muscle Tension

Learn different massage techniques to relieve stress and muscle tension in your pet, improving their physical and emotional well-being.

There's no doubt that our pets have a very special place in our lives. They provide us with companionship, unconditional love and teach us the true meaning of loyalty. This is why we want to take care of them in the best possible way. In addition to proper nutrition and regular exercise, therapeutic massage has become an invaluable tool to strengthen the special bond we share with our pets.

Like humans, animals can also suffer from stress and muscle tension. Fortunately, there are several massage techniques that can help them alleviate these ailments, promoting their physical and emotional well-being. In addition, therapeutic massage can offer other benefits such as improving circulation, reducing inflammation and strengthening your pet's immune system.

One of the most popular techniques for relieving muscle tension in dogs is deep tissue massage. This type of massage focuses on the deepest muscles and connective tissues, releasing accumulated tension and improving flexibility. To do this, you must apply firm but gentle pressure with the palms of your hands or fingers, following the direction of the muscles. Remember to pay special attention to areas where your pet tends to accumulate the most tension, such as the neck, back and hind legs.

In the case of cats, gentle, rhythmic massage is a very effective technique for relieving both stress and muscle tension. Cats are very sensitive animals, so it's important to adapt the massage to your preferred style and pace. Start by gently stroking your skin with slow, circular motions. Watch how your cat reacts and adapt to its needs. You can also use your fingers to gently press specific areas, such as the base of the tail or the base of the ears.

Rabbits, on the other hand, can benefit greatly from stretching massages. These massages help to relax muscles and joints, relieving tension accumulated after intense physical activities or periods of stress. To perform a stretching massage on your rabbit, gently stroke its back and then, gently but firmly, extend each of its legs forward, following the natural direction of the muscles. Make sure you don't exert too much pressure and listen to your rabbit's signals to ensure comfort.

Every pet is unique and may require different massage techniques to relieve stress and muscle tension. Observe your pet, pay attention to their needs and adapt the massage to their comfort. Remember that therapeutic massage, in addition to improving your physical well-being, creates an environment of harmony and special connection between you and your pet.

In the second half of this chapter, we will continue to explore massage techniques to relieve stress and muscle tension in our pets. Each animal is unique and may require a different approach, but always keeping their physical and emotional well-being in mind.

For birds, an effective massage technique is wing massage. This type of massage can help relieve the stress and muscle tension that can result from flying or being in tight spaces. Start by applying gentle pressure to your bird's wings, following the direction of the feathers. You can also use gentle stretching techniques, making sure you don't exert too much pressure. Watch how your pet reacts and adapt to their comfort.

For rodents, such as hamsters or guinea pigs, tummy massage can be very beneficial in relieving muscle tension and promoting their overall well-being. To perform this massage, place your rodent on your hand, face down, and apply gentle pressure to its belly with your fingers. Make circular and gentle movements, listening to your pet's signals and adapting to their comfort.

Reptiles can also benefit from massage techniques to relieve stress and muscle tension. For a relaxing reptile massage, first, make sure you have a warm and calm environment to make them feel comfortable. Then gently caress your body with slow, gentle movements, avoiding applying too much pressure. Watch how your pet reacts and adapt to their cues to ensure their well-being.

It is important to remember that therapeutic massage for pets should be gradual and gentle. You should always pay attention to your pet's reactions and signals. If at any time you seem uncomfortable or stressed, stop the massage and try another, more gentle technique. The key is to strengthen the special bond you share with your pet and to promote their physical and emotional well-being.

In addition to massage, you can also complement your pet's care with additional therapies such as aromatherapy or music therapy. These therapies can help reduce stress and promote relaxation in your pet. However, it's important to remember that every animal is unique and may have different preferences and reactions to these complementary therapies.

Remember that the main objective of therapeutic massage is to provide your pet with a special moment of relaxation and care. By dedicating yourself to learning and practicing these techniques, you'll be strengthening the special bond you share with your pet and improving their quality of life.

In summary, in this chapter we learned different massage techniques to relieve stress and muscle tension in our pets. Each animal will require a different approach, but we must always prioritize their physical and emotional well-being. Remember to pay attention to your pet's cues and adapt the massage to their needs. Therapeutic massage, along with other complementary therapies, can be a valuable tool to strengthen the special bond we share with our pets and promote their health and happiness.

Continue to explore and experiment with these massage techniques and discover which ones work best for your pet. I'm sure you'll enjoy unique moments of connection and relaxation with your faithful companion!

Well-being and happiness for you and your pet. Go ahead!

Chapter 7: Massages to Increase Flexibility and Mobility

Explore how therapeutic massages can help your pet stay agile, improve their range of motion and prevent injuries.

Our furry friends bring us unparalleled joy and companionship. But, just like us, they can suffer from muscle aches, stiffness, and even injuries. Therapeutic massages are a great way to help your pet stay agile and fit, improving their flexibility and mobility.

When it comes to our beloved animals, we often wonder what we can do to promote their well-being and keep them healthy. Therapeutic massages are an ancient technique that offers many benefits for our pets. Beyond being a mere act of caring, massages can have a significant impact on your overall health and well-being.

Therapeutic massages have the ability to release muscle tension, promote blood circulation and trigger relaxation. These benefits translate into greater flexibility and mobility for your faithful companion. In addition, massages can also help prevent injuries and relieve existing pain.

Imagine your pet energetic and full of vitality, enjoying every moment to the fullest. Therapeutic massages can contribute to this state of well-being. Through specific techniques, we can work on the muscles of our pets, loosening accumulated tensions and promoting a greater range of motion.

During the massage, it's crucial that your pet is in a calm and relaxed environment. You can create an enabling space by using soft lights, soft music, and a comfortable surface to lie on. Make sure your furry friend is comfortable and calm before you start.

Start the massage by gently stroking your pet's body, paying special attention to their muscles and joints. You can use circular movements and gentle pressure to relax tense muscles. As you progress, watch how your pet reacts, adjusting the intensity and pace of your movements according to their needs.

As you become more familiar with massage therapy, you'll be able to identify specific areas that require additional attention. For example, if you notice stiffness in your dog's hind legs, you can spend more time massaging that particular area, using techniques that help to relax the muscles and improve their flexibility.

In addition to working directly on the muscles, therapeutic massages can also be beneficial to your pet's circulatory and lymphatic system. Stimulating these systems can contribute to a better elimination of toxins and waste accumulated in the body, helping to prevent unwanted diseases and inflammation.

Always remember to respect your pet's limits during the massage. If at any time you show discomfort or rejection, stop the session and see a veterinarian. Every animal is different and may have specific preferences and needs.

In short, therapeutic massages can be an invaluable tool to strengthen the special bond we have with our pets. Not only do they contribute to your physical well-being, they also promote a state of relaxation and calm. Over time, you'll notice your pet becoming more agile and enjoying greater flexibility and mobility.

The second part of this chapter will reveal new and exciting aspects of therapeutic massage for pets. We'll continue to explore how this technique can help you recover from injuries and how to adapt massages to the different stages of your pet's life. Stay tuned and be surprised by the following benefits that we will discover together!

Once you've practiced therapeutic massages on your pet and become familiar with the basic techniques, you can begin to explore more advanced ways to improve their flexibility and mobility. In this second part of the chapter, you'll discover how to adapt massages to the different stages of your pet's life and how this technique can help them recover from injuries.

When it comes to therapeutic massages for pets, it's important to consider the specific needs of your furry companion. For example, if you have a puppy, it's essential that the massage be gentle and gentle, as their body is still developing. Pay attention to their growth and adapt massage techniques as they grow.

For adult dogs, therapeutic massages can be a valuable tool to maintain their flexibility and prevent injuries. The aging process can lead to stiffness and even arthritis in pets. Regular massages can help relieve these symptoms and promote better mobility in muscles and joints.

When massaging your pet, be sure to pay special attention to areas where there have been injuries or where there is increased muscle tension. For example, if your dog has had a leg injury, you can work on that specific area with gentle, circular movements to aid in his recovery.

In addition to massages, consider complementing the treatment with other methods that promote your pet's flexibility and mobility. For example, you can do gentle stretching before and after massages to stretch your muscles and increase their range of motion.

Another important aspect to consider is the individuality of each animal. Every pet has their specific preferences and needs, so it's essential to be attentive to their reaction during the massage. If your pet shows discomfort or rejection at any time, stop the session and see a veterinarian. Remember that your main objective is to provide well-being and relief, so the comfort and convenience of your pet should always be a priority.

As you continue to practice therapeutic massages on your pet, you may notice an improvement in their flexibility and mobility. Your furry companion will enjoy a greater range of motion and will feel freer and more agile. Massages not only contribute to his physical well-being, but they also promote a state of relaxation and calm, which will further strengthen the special bond you have with him.

In conclusion, therapeutic massages can be an invaluable tool to improve your pet's flexibility and mobility. Adapting techniques to your age and specific needs will ensure effective and safe treatment. Don't forget to supplement massages with other methods, such as gentle stretching, to maximize the benefits. Enjoy this special connection with your pet and be surprised by the results you will achieve together!

Remember that the well-being and health of your pet is an important responsibility. It is always advisable to consult a veterinarian before starting any new treatment or technique. Your veterinarian will be able to provide professional guidance and adapt therapeutic massages to your pet's specific needs.

You'll continue to learn more about therapeutic massages and how to adapt them to the different stages of your pet's life in the coming chapters. Don't miss out on the exciting techniques and tips we'll share to help you care for and strengthen the health of your faithful friend. Stay tuned and keep enjoying the benefits of massages for your pet!

Chapter 8: Massages to Relieve Pain and Inflammation

Learn massage techniques that can relieve pain and reduce inflammation in your pet, promoting their health and well-being.

The well-being of our pets is a priority for all animal lovers. We want them to be happy, healthy and free from any discomfort they may experience. Therapeutic massages have become an effective tool for relieving pain and reducing inflammation in pets, allowing them to have a better quality of life.

Therapeutic massage not only provides physical comfort to our pets, it also strengthens the special bond we share with them. Through loving touch and skillful hands, we can connect deeply with our furry friends and provide them with the care they need.

When it comes to relieving pain and inflammation, it's essential to understand the proper techniques to apply in every situation. First of all, you should keep in mind that therapeutic massage does not replace professional veterinary care. If your pet is experiencing persistent pain or swelling, it's essential to consult a veterinarian before implementing any massage technique.

One of the most effective massage techniques for relieving pain and reducing inflammation is deep tissue massage. This type of massage focuses on reaching the deepest layers of muscles and tissues, releasing accumulated tension and promoting blood circulation. To perform this massage, use slow, firm movements, gradually applying pressure and working on problem areas.

Another beneficial technique for relieving pain and reducing inflammation is compression massage. It involves applying gentle, sustained pressure to the affected muscles and joints. This technique helps improve circulation and reduce muscle tension, thus relieving any pain or inflammation present in your pet.

In addition to these techniques, there are different complementary methods you can use to relieve pain and reduce inflammation in your pet. Using essential oils, such as lavender or chamomile, can provide additional relief and promote relaxation.

It's important to remember that every pet is unique and may respond differently to therapeutic massages. Some may relax quickly and enjoy the experience, while others may need more time to feel comfortable. Watch your pet's signs and adapt massage techniques to their needs and preferences.

In the next chapter, we'll explore other techniques and methods for relieving pain and reducing inflammation in your pets. You'll continue to discover new ways to strengthen the special bond with your furry friend, while improving their health and well-being.

Remember, therapeutic massage is a powerful tool to promote the health and well-being of our pets. Keep exploring the wonders that massage can offer and be amazed at the results you'll get!

One of these methods is the use of acupressure. Acupressure is a technique based on traditional Chinese medicine that involves applying pressure to specific points on the body to promote balance and circulation of vital energy.

There are acupressure points that are especially beneficial for relieving pain and reducing inflammation in pets. For example, gently massaging the spot at the base of the ear can help relieve joint pain and promote relaxation throughout your pet's body. Another important point is at the base of the hind leg, just below the knee. Massaging this area can help reduce inflammation and relieve joint pain.

Always remember to be gentle and respectful when working with acupressure points, and if you have any questions or lack of knowledge, consult a professional in traditional Chinese medicine or veterinary acupuncture.

Another technique that can be beneficial is massage with a heat applicator. Heat can help relax muscles, improve blood circulation, and relieve pain and inflammation in pets. Use a heat applicator designed especially for animals, and follow the instructions for use to avoid burns or discomfort for your pet. This technique can be especially useful in cases of chronic pain or joint stiffness in older pets.

In addition to the techniques mentioned, stretching can also be beneficial in relieving pain and reducing inflammation in pets. Gentle, controlled stretching can help improve your pet's flexibility and mobility, relieving tension and discomfort in muscles and joints. Always be aware of your pet's physical limitations and avoid any sudden or pain-causing movement.

It's critical to remember that every pet is unique and may respond differently to different massage techniques. Some may enjoy certain techniques more than others, and it's important to respect their preferences and limitations. If at any time your pet shows signs of discomfort or discomfort during the massage, stop the session and consult a veterinarian.

To conclude, I want to remind you of the importance of consulting a veterinarian if your pet has persistent pain or inflammation. Therapeutic massage can be an effective tool for alleviating these symptoms, but proper diagnosis and treatment are always necessary.

Keep exploring the wonders of therapeutic massage and enjoy strengthening the special bond with your pet. Remember that, as responsible owners, we have the ability to provide them with the care and love they need to live full and healthy lives. Your pet will be grateful for every moment of well-being that you provide through your loving hands!

(This is the end of chapter 8. We hope you've enjoyed this guide to therapeutic massages to relieve pain and inflammation in pets. If you're interested in learning more and going deeper into the topic, don't hesitate to check out additional resources on massage therapy for pets. We wish you the best on your path to the health and well-being of your furry friend!)

Chapter 9: Massages to Strengthen the Immune System

Learn how therapeutic massage can help strengthen your pet's immune system, keeping it healthy and resistant to diseases.

The health of our pets is a priority for all responsible pet owners. We want to make sure they're happy, active, and disease-free. In addition to good nutrition and regular exercise, there is a highly beneficial and comforting technique to improve the health of our beloved pets: therapeutic massages.

Therapeutic massage is not only a way to relax our pets, but it also has significant benefits for their immune system. This chapter will focus on how these massages can strengthen your furry companion's immune response, keeping him strong and healthy.

The immune system of our pets plays a crucial role in protecting and defending their body against diseases and infectious agents. However, factors such as stress, poor diet or lack of physical activity can weaken their immune system, leaving them more exposed to diseases and other health challenges.

This is where therapeutic massages come into play. The gentle, rhythmic movements applied during a massage have the ability to boost your pet's immune response. By promoting blood circulation and lymphatic flow, massages help eliminate toxins and stimulate the production of white blood cells, which are essential for fighting diseases.

In addition to strengthening the immune system, therapeutic massages also improve your pet's overall circulation. This means that nutrients and oxygen reach tissues and organs more efficiently, contributing to their overall well-being. A healthy circulatory system is essential for your pet to recover quickly from illnesses and injuries.

Another important benefit of massages is its ability to reduce stress in pets. All pets, just like humans, experience stressful situations in their daily lives. Chronic stress can affect your pet's immune system, weakening it and making it more susceptible to diseases. Therapeutic massages relieve stress by releasing endorphins, the so-called "happiness hormones", which help to relax and calm your furry companion.

It is important to note that therapeutic massages should not replace veterinary care, but complement it. You should always check with your veterinarian before starting any therapeutic massage program for your pet, especially if your pet has a specific condition or injury.

In short, therapeutic massages can be a powerful tool for strengthening your pet's immune system. They boost circulation, improve immune response and reduce stress, all of which help keep your furry companion healthy and resistant to diseases.

In the second part of this chapter, we'll explore specific massage techniques you can use to strengthen your pet's immune system. We will continue our journey through the fascinating world of therapeutic massages for pets and provide you with practical tips for carrying out this wonderful form of care at home. Stay tuned! Your pet will thank you. The second part of this chapter will immerse us in the various therapeutic massage techniques you can use to strengthen your pet's immune system. These techniques focus on specific areas of your furry companion's body to further boost their immune response and promote their overall well-being.

One of the most effective techniques is pressure point massage. These spots are found all over your pet's body and are connected to different organs and systems. By applying pressure to these points, blood circulation and lymph flow can be stimulated, strengthening the immune system and improving overall health.

To perform pressure point massage, you must first familiarize yourself with the location of these points on your pet's body. They are generally found in areas such as the base of the skull, the spine, the legs and the area of the abdomen. With gentle but firm movements, apply pressure to each of these points for a few seconds and then release. Repeat this process on different areas of your pet's body for better results.

Another technique you can use is deep tissue massage. This type of massage focuses on the deeper layers of muscles and connective tissues, helping to release tension and promote greater circulation of blood and nutrients. Deep tissue massage

It also stimulates the production of collagen, a protein essential for tissue repair and disease resistance.

For a deep tissue massage, place your hands on your pet's muscles with firm but painless pressure. Then, make slow, deep movements, working in the direction of the muscle fibers. As you progress, you can apply a little more pressure to reach the deeper layers of the tissue. Always remember to be attentive to your pet's reactions and adjust the pressure accordingly.

In addition to these techniques, you can also incorporate the use of essential oils during therapeutic massages. Some oils, such as lavender or chamomile, have relaxing and anti-inflammatory properties that can help strengthen your pet's immune system. Always be sure to dilute essential oils with a base oil, such as coconut or almond, before applying them to your pet's skin.

Remember that every pet is unique and may have different preferences and needs. It's important to watch how your furry companion reacts during the massage and adjust techniques and pressure accordingly. Always look for your pet's well-being and comfort throughout the process.

In conclusion, therapeutic massages can be a powerful tool to strengthen your pet's immune system. Whether through pressure point massage, deep tissue massage or the addition of essential oils, these massages promote circulation, improve immune response and reduce stress on your furry companion. Don't hesitate to start using these techniques at home and see how your pet benefits from them. A strong immune system and a healthy pet will thank you!

Chapter 10: Massage as part of the daily routine

The well-being of our pets is of the utmost importance to us, their owners. We want to ensure that they are healthy, happy and balanced at every stage of their life. This is why we must consider therapeutic massage as a powerful tool to strengthen your long-term well-being.

Learning how to incorporate therapeutic massage into your pet's daily routine will not only allow you to maintain a special bond with them, but it will also contribute to improving their quality of life. The benefits of this practice go beyond relaxation and the release of tension. Therapeutic massage can relieve muscle aches, reduce anxiety, improve blood circulation and strengthen the immune system of your faithful companion.

The first step in incorporating massage into your pet's daily routine is to establish a calm and relaxed environment. Find a comfortable place where both of you feel relaxed and free of distractions. It can be in your living room, in the garden, or in any other quiet space in your home. Make sure you have all the necessary items on hand, such as oils or massage creams specifically formulated for pets, soft pillows or blankets, and toys that can provide them with comfort.

Once you've created the right environment, it's time to get started with therapeutic massage. Remember that the main objective is to provide your pet with a pleasant and relaxing experience, so it is essential to respect their comfort and limits. Start by gently stroking her body, paying attention to any tension or sensitivity you can detect. If your pet shows signs of discomfort or discomfort, stop immediately and adjust the pressure or intensity of your movements.

When performing the therapeutic massage, consider the different areas of your pet's body that can benefit from this type of stimulation. He pays special attention to his muscles, joints and spine, performing circular, kneading and gentle stretching movements. See how your pet responds to each technique and adjust your approach to their individual needs.

Therapeutic massage is not only effective for your pet's body, but also for their mind. During the massage session, take the opportunity to strengthen the emotional bond with your faithful companion. Speak in a soft, comforting voice, use loving words, and spend quality time with your pet. This emotional connection will further strengthen the positive impact of massage on your overall well-being.

As you become more familiar with the practice of therapeutic massage, you can incorporate it as an essential part of your pet's daily routine. Establishing a regular schedule for massage sessions will help create a predictable and comforting environment. Watch your pet eagerly look forward to each session, anticipating the benefits of this practice.

Remember that therapeutic massage can be a mutually rewarding experience for both you and your pet. In addition to the physical and emotional benefits it provides, the practice of massage will allow you to dedicate exclusive time to your faithful companion, thus strengthening the special bond that unites them.

Read on in the second part of this chapter to discover specific therapeutic massage techniques and how to adapt them to your pet's individual needs! During this second part of the chapter, I'll teach you specific therapeutic massage techniques that you can adapt to your pet's individual needs. These techniques will allow you to further improve their overall well-being and strengthen the special bond that unites them.

An effective and pleasant therapeutic massage technique is kneading. To perform this technique, you must hold your pet's muscles gently between your hands and apply constant pressure while gently massaging them in circular motions. Kneading helps to relax tense muscles and promotes better blood circulation. Remember to adjust the pressure according to your pet's comfort and pay attention to their responses to make sure they are enjoying the massage.

Another useful technique is gentle stretching. As you massage your pet, you can gently stretch their limbs and muscles. These stretches help improve your pet's flexibility and mobility, preventing possible injuries or muscle stiffness. Remember to stretch gently and gradually, avoiding forcing your pet at any time.

If your pet shows signs of anxiety or tension, you can use the pressure point technique to relieve these symptoms. Pressure points are located in different areas of the body and applying gentle pressure to these points can help release accumulated tension. However, it's essential to consult with a professional before attempting this technique to make sure you're doing it correctly and not causing any harm to your pet.

In addition to specific massage techniques, it's important to pay attention to the signs and signals your pet is giving you during the session. Watch their body language and reactions to adjust your approach to their individual needs. If your pet shows signs of discomfort or discomfort, stop immediately and use a milder technique or switch to another area of the body that may be more pleasant for them.

Remember that therapeutic massage should not replace proper veterinary care. You should always consult a trusted professional with any concerns about your pet's health. Therapeutic massage can complement veterinary care, but it is not a substitute.

Finally, I encourage you to take advantage of each massage session to further strengthen the emotional bond with your pet. Speak in a soft, comforting voice, give her words of encouragement, and show your love and affection to her. These quality moments together will not only improve the massage experience, but they will also strengthen your relationship and mutual trust.

As you continue to incorporate therapeutic massage into your pet's daily routine, you'll notice how it benefits from this practice. Massage will not only improve your physical well-being, but it will also strengthen the emotional connection between the two. Enjoy this time together and always remember to adapt the massage to your pet's individual needs.

I hope you enjoyed this chapter on how to incorporate therapeutic massage into your pet's daily routine. Read on to learn more about how to maintain long-term well-being and discover other important aspects of caring for your pets at. Until then, enjoy your massage sessions and continue to strengthen the special bond with your faithful companion!

Chapter 11: Massage for Dogs

Learn about specific therapeutic massage techniques for dogs and how to adapt them to different breeds and needs.

Therapeutic massage can be a wonderful way to strengthen the special bond we have with our pets. Dogs, just like us, can greatly benefit from massage techniques, which not only provide them with relaxation and stress relief, but also promote their physical and emotional well-being.

To perform an effective therapeutic massage for your dog, it is important to know the specific techniques and know how to adapt them to the individual needs of your furry companion. Each breed and each dog has different characteristics, so it is essential to adjust the massage according to their size, age and state of health.

Let's start with the basic massage techniques you can apply to your dog. The first of these is kneading, which involves gently pressing and releasing the muscles using circular movements with the hands. This type of massage is ideal for relaxing tense muscles and releasing the tension built up in your dog's body.

Another very beneficial technique is surface gliding, which involves gently stroking your dog's coat in the direction of hair growth. This type of massage is ideal for stimulating blood circulation and relaxing your dog.

Percussion massage is another technique you can use on your dog. It consists of gently hitting your pet's body with your hands in rhythmic and gentle movements. This type of massage helps to stimulate your dog's muscles and reflexes, promoting a sense of well-being.

It is important to mention that each dog breed may require different approaches when applying therapeutic massage. For example, small breed dogs such as the Chihuahua or the Yorkshire Terrier may need a softer and more delicate massage because of their size and fragility. On the other hand, large breed dogs such as the Labrador Retriever or the German Shepherd may need a firmer and deeper massage due to their robust muscle structure.

In addition to adapting massage techniques to different breeds, it's also important to consider the individual needs of each dog. Some dogs may have specific areas that require more attention, such as joints or tense muscles. Pay special attention to these areas during the massage, applying gentle but firm movements to provide relief and relaxation.

Remember, it is always advisable to seek the guidance of a professional in therapeutic massage for dogs if you have questions or if your dog has a particular health condition. A trained canine masseur can provide personalized advice and techniques for your furry friend's well-being.

In the next chapter, we'll explore specialized massage techniques for dogs with specific needs, such as older dogs, dogs recovering from injuries, or dogs with anxiety. We'll discover how to adapt massage to these situations and how to provide maximum benefit to our beloved pets.

The second half of the chapter covers specialized massage techniques for dogs with specific needs. It is important to note that we must always adapt the massage to the individual needs of our dog and seek the guidance of a professional if we have questions or if our dog has a particular health condition.

For older dogs, massage can be a wonderful way to relieve the aches and pains associated with old age. Older dogs often experience stiff joints and may have tight muscles due to aging. For them, it is advisable to use gentle and delicate massage techniques, focusing on areas such as the hips, knees and spine.

Therapeutic massage can also be beneficial for dogs recovering from injuries. In these cases, it's important to work together with the vet and follow the specific instructions to ensure that you don't cause any additional harm. Massage can help improve circulation, reduce inflammation, and promote the healing of damaged tissues. It is essential to apply soft and firm movements, avoiding any area that is inflamed or sensitive.

For dogs with anxiety, massage can be an invaluable tool to help them relax and find calm. Gentle, soothing massage techniques, such as kneading and superficial gliding, can be especially helpful in these cases. It is important to create a calm and safe environment for the massage, avoiding any situation that could increase our dog's anxiety.

In addition to specific techniques for older dogs, recovering from injuries or with anxiety, there are other ways to adapt massage to the individual needs of our pets. For example, some dogs may enjoy head and neck massage, while others like leg or lower back massage more.

It is essential to pay attention to the signals that our dog gives us during the massage. Observing their body language and reaction will help us determine if we're applying the right pressure, if we're making the right movements, and if our dog feels comfortable and relaxed. We must always respect our dog's limits and adjust the massage according to their individual preferences and needs.

In short, therapeutic massage for dogs is an excellent way to strengthen the special bond we have with our pets. Knowing the specific techniques and adapting them to the individual needs of our dog is essential to provide them with the physical and emotional benefits that massage can offer. Always remember to seek the advice of a professional if you have questions or if your dog has a particular health condition.

Continue to learn and explore the wonderful techniques of therapeutic massage to strengthen the bond with your faithful canine companion!

Chapter 12: Massage for cats

Discover the ideal therapeutic massage techniques for cats and how to address their unique sensitivities and preferences.

Cats are beautiful and enigmatic creatures, known for their independent and mysterious behavior. Although they may seem reserved, cats also need physical care and attention to maintain their overall well-being. A great way to strengthen the special bond you have with your feline and help it stay healthy is through therapeutic massage. In this chapter, we'll explore ideal massage techniques for cats and how to address their unique sensitivity and preferences.

Before you start massaging your cat, it's important to understand their body language and comfort signals. It is essential to establish a calm and relaxed environment so that your feline feels comfortable during the massage session. See if your cat is relaxed, with its tail in a neutral position and its ears facing forward. If you notice any signs of discomfort, such as an arched loin or a lowered tail, stop the massage and give your cat space.

When you start the massage, use gentle, slow movements to get your cat used to this new experience. Start by gently massaging your head and neck, using circular, gentle pressing movements. This will help to relax the muscles and release accumulated tension.

As you continue the massage, pay special attention to areas where your cat can accumulate the most tension, such as the lower back area and hind legs. Use gentle sliding and kneading movements to release tension and promote blood circulation in these areas. If you notice any spots of tenderness, apply softer pressure or adjust the technique until you find your cat's comfort.

Remember that every cat is different and there may be variations in their massage preferences. Some cats may enjoy a more energetic massage, while others may prefer softer touches. Observe your cat's reactions and adjust the intensity and technique according to their individual needs.

During the massage, you can also use oils or lotions specifically formulated for cats. These products can help moisturize your feline's skin and make the experience even more relaxing. However, it's important to use products specially designed for cats, as some common ingredients in human products can be toxic to them. Always check with your vet before using any product on your cat.

As you complete the first half of this chapter, remember that therapeutic massage can be a beneficial experience for both you and your cat. Establish a regular massage routine and enjoy this special time together. In the second part of this chapter, we'll explore advanced massage techniques for cats and how to adapt them to the specific needs of your beloved feline.

So far, we have learned the fundamental basics of therapeutic massage for cats. Now, get ready to discover more specialized techniques that will allow you to deepen the well-being of your feline companion. Remember to maintain a calm environment and respect your cat's limits during the massage. Don't miss the second part of this chapter, where we'll unveil the secrets of feline relaxation! In the second part of this chapter, we will delve into more specialized therapeutic massage techniques for cats, which will allow you to continue strengthening the special bond you have with your feline.

An advanced massage technique for cats is facial massage. Start by gently stroking the area around your cat's eyes and cheekbones with circular, gentle pressing movements. Pay attention to your cat's reactions and make sure he's comfortable. Some cats may enjoy the gentle stimulation of these movements, while others may prefer a lighter touch. As you practice facial massage, you can also use gentle sliding movements along your cat's cheeks to further relax the facial muscles.

Another useful technique for addressing accumulated tension in the area of the back and hind legs is deep tissue massage. This type of massage focuses on releasing deep tension in your cat's muscles and connective tissues. Use deeper, slower pressing movements along your back and hind legs, focusing on areas where you feel the most resistance or tension. Remember that it's important to be careful and adapt the pressure to your cat's comfort. If you ever feel uncomfortable or show signs of pain, stop the massage immediately.

In addition to massage techniques, you can also incorporate the use of essential oils specially formulated for cats. Some essential oils, such as lavender or chamomile, are known for their relaxing properties and can help create a peaceful environment during the massage. However, before using essential oils, be sure to research what oils are safe for cats and always dilute them properly before use. Remember that every cat is unique and can react differently to essential oils, so it's essential to carefully observe your cat's reactions during the massage.

At the end of the massage session, be sure to allow your cat to rest and relax. You can offer him cool water and a quiet place where he can rest after the massage experience. See if your cat shows signs of relaxation, such as closing its eyes and stretching comfortably.

Remember that therapeutic massage for cats is a wonderful way to strengthen the bond between you and your feline, while promoting their physical and emotional well-being. As you continue to practice these techniques, you'll be creating an environment of trust and love with your cat, helping them to stay healthy and happy.

In this second part of the chapter, we have explored more specialized massage techniques for cats, such as facial massage and deep tissue massage. We have also mentioned the possibility of using essential oils specifically formulated for cats. Always remember to adapt the techniques and pressure of the massage to the individual needs of your feline.

We hope you have enjoyed these advanced massage techniques and that you will put them into practice to further strengthen the special bond with your feline companion. In the next chapter, we'll explore other forms of physical care for cats that will complement therapeutic massage. Don't miss the continuation of this guide dedicated to the well-being of your beloved pet!

Chapter 13: Massage for birds and other small animals

L earn how to safely and effectively use therapeutic massage on birds and other small animals to promote their well-being.

Therapeutic massage, an ancient technique used to calm the body and mind, is not only beneficial for human beings, but also for our beloved pets. In this chapter, we'll explore how to safely and effectively apply therapeutic massage to birds and other small animals, thus strengthening the special bond we share with them.

Relaxation and well-being are essential for both humans and animals. Through therapeutic massage, we can provide physical and emotional relief to our pets, helping them to maintain a state of calm and inner peace. However, we must remember that each animal species has its own needs and anatomical particularities. Therefore, it is essential to properly adapt our massage techniques to the specific characteristics of each animal.

When it comes to birds and other small animals, we must consider their physical fragility. Using gentle pressure and gentle movements is essential to avoid injury. Before starting any massage session, it's important to ensure that the environment is calm and free from any distractions. Some animals may feel uncomfortable or unsafe at first, so it's essential to provide them with a serene and familiar environment.

To get started, place your bird or small animal on a soft, padded surface. Make sure they feel comfortable and relaxed before starting the massage session. Observe their body language: if they are receiving the massage in a positive way, they will demonstrate this through signs such as relaxing their muscles and a calm attitude.

Before touching your pet directly, start by gently stroking their plumage or fur with slow, loving movements. This will help them relax and get used to your presence. As you progress through your massage session, pay special attention to areas of your body that are tense or sore. Make circular and gentle movements in these areas, applying light pressure according to your comfort.

Remember that each bird and small animal may have different preferences when it comes to the areas they enjoy being petted or massaged. Some may find paw massage pleasurable, while others may prefer the chest or back area. Watch their reaction carefully and adapt your techniques according to their comfort and well-being.

As you continue with the massage session, keep an upbeat and loving attitude. Your pet senses your emotions and, if you stay relaxed and happy, this will help create a positive environment for both of you. Don't forget to express your love and gratitude to your pet during the process. Therapeutic massage not only strengthens the bond with your pet, but it also promotes their overall health and well-being.

Massage for birds and other small animals is a wonderful tool for providing care and love. In the second part of this chapter, we'll explore some additional techniques and specific exercises to maximize the benefits of therapeutic massage on these adorable, feathered, small-sized creatures. Get ready to discover new ways to strengthen the special connection you have with your pet! As you continue with the therapeutic massage session with your bird or small animal, it's important to remember that each pet is unique and may have different preferences in terms of the areas that enjoy being petted or massaged. Watch their reaction carefully and adapt your techniques according to their comfort and well-being.

Some animals may find massaging the paws, where many nerve endings are concentrated, pleasurable. To massage this area, use gentle, circular movements on each finger, paying special attention to the spaces between them. If your bird or animal shows resistance or discomfort, it's important to respect their limits and focus on other parts of the body where they feel most comfortable.

The chest area can also be a pleasant area for massage for some birds and small animals. Use gentle, rhythmic movements, stroking from the base of the neck to the bottom of the chest. If you notice that your pet is enjoying this massage, you can apply gentle pressure in circular motions to encourage relaxation and well-being.

Another area that many animals enjoy is the back. Slide your hands from the base of the neck to the tail, applying gentle pressure in gentle, circular motions. Pay attention to any tension or stiffness you may perceive and adjust pressure and movements accordingly.

Remember that therapeutic massage has not only physical benefits, but also emotional ones. During the massage session, maintain an optimistic and loving attitude towards your pet. Physical contact and positive attention will strengthen the special bond you have with her and will help create a relaxed and safe environment.

Also, take the opportunity to express your love and gratitude to your pet. Speak in a soft, comforting voice, offering words of encouragement and congratulations. Your pet will feel your love and care, which will help create a positive experience during the massage.

Remember that emotional well-being and relaxation are essential for both humans and animals. Through therapeutic massage, you can provide your pet with an oasis of calm and inner peace. As you continue to explore and experiment with different massage techniques, always keep the individual needs and preferences of your bird or small animal in mind.

Therapeutic massage for birds and other small animals is a wonderful tool to strengthen the special bond we share with them. As you pamper your pet with this loving care, you're not only promoting their health and well-being, but you're also cultivating a relationship based on love, trust, and deep connection.

In conclusion, therapeutic massage can be an enriching experience for both you and your pet. Through gentle, circular and loving movements, you can help your bird or small animal find a sense of relaxation and well-being. Remember to adapt your techniques to the specific needs of each pet and use this opportunity to strengthen your special bond. Don't hesitate to continue exploring new ways to pamper and care for your adorable feathered companion or small animal!

Chapter 14: Massage for Older Pets

Learn how therapeutic massage can benefit older pets, relieving pain and improving their quality of life.

At the stage of our pets' lives when they begin to age, it is essential to provide them with the right care so that they continue to enjoy an active and full life. Like humans, pets can also experience aches and pains associated with aging, such as arthritis and muscle stiffness. Fortunately, therapeutic massage can be an effective tool to alleviate these ailments and improve the quality of life of our faithful companions.

One of the main benefits of therapeutic massage for older pets is its ability to relieve pain. Gentle, controlled massage helps to stimulate blood circulation and reduce inflammation in the joints, which in turn decreases pain and discomfort. This is especially beneficial for those dogs and cats that suffer from arthritis, as massage can help increase their mobility and flexibility.

In addition to relieving pain, therapeutic massage also offers a number of benefits in terms of overall well-being. During the massage session, endorphins are released, hormones responsible for generating a feeling of relaxation and happiness. Not only do these endorphins help reduce stress and anxiety in older pets, they also strengthen the special bond we have with them. As our pets age, it's critical to provide them with care that makes them feel loved, cared for, and still full of vitality.

Therapeutic massage can also have a positive impact on the immune system of older pets. As they age, their immune system can weaken, leaving them more vulnerable to diseases and conditions. However, through massage, we can boost their immune system and help them maintain good overall health. It's important to emphasize that massage is not a substitute for proper veterinary care, but it can effectively complement it.

In addition, therapeutic massage promotes muscle relaxation and the release of accumulated tension. Older pets tend to experience muscle and joint stiffness due to decreased physical activity and loss of elasticity. By using specific massage techniques, we can loosen those tight muscles and allow our pets to move more easily.

In short, therapeutic massage can make a big difference in the lives of our older pets. It relieves pain, improves mobility, strengthens the bond with them and promotes their overall well-being. If you're an older pet owner, consider including regular massage sessions in your daily routine. As guardians of these special beings, it is our duty to provide them with the care and attention they deserve so that they can enjoy a life full of joy and comfort.

To be continued... Therapeutic massage not only relieves pain and improves mobility for older pets, but it can also have positive effects on their mood and emotional well-being. It's common for older pets to experience changes in their behavior, such as irritability, anxiety, or depression. Therapeutic massage can help calm these emotions and promote a state of relaxation and tranquility.

During the massage session, a calm and safe environment is created where pets can feel protected and loved. This is especially important for those pets that have experienced loss, such as that of a life partner or changes in their environment. Massage can provide comfort and emotional support, strengthening the special bond between them and their owners.

In addition, therapeutic massage stimulates the release of wellness hormones, such as serotonin and oxytocin. Not only do these hormones improve the mood of our pets, they can also help lower blood pressure and stress. Massage is a natural and effective way to promote an overall sense of well-being in our older pets.

Another important aspect of therapeutic massage for older pets is its ability to stimulate blood circulation and improve the functionality of internal organs. With aging, it's common for pets to experience health problems such as decreased kidney or cardiovascular function. Massage can help improve circulation and oxygen flow through the body, thus promoting the internal health of our pets.

In addition to the physical and emotional benefits, therapeutic massage can also be an excellent opportunity to detect any changes in the health of our older pets. During the massage session, we can look at your skin, coat, muscles and joints for any abnormalities or signs of illness. By being aware of these changes, we can take preventive measures or consult our trusted veterinarian for a proper diagnosis.

It is important to note that therapeutic massage for older pets must be performed by a trained professional or under the supervision of an animal massage expert. Each pet is unique and may have specific needs, so it is essential to perform the massage properly and safely.

In conclusion, therapeutic massage can be a very beneficial tool to improve the quality of life of our older pets. Not only does it relieve pain and improve mobility, but it also promotes their emotional well-being and strengthens our special connection with them. By including regular massage sessions in the daily routine of our older pets, we are providing the care and attention they deserve at this stage of their lives.

Remember, as responsible owners, it's our responsibility to take care of our older pets and provide them with a full and happy life. Therapeutic massage is just one of the many ways we can do it. Continue to learn and explore new ways to care for and strengthen the bond with our pets on their path to aging. Their unconditional love and companionship have accompanied us throughout the years, and it is our duty to repay them with the love and care they deserve.

Thank you for joining us in this chapter on massage for older pets. Keep learning and discovering new ways to enrich the lives of your faithful companions. Until the next adventure in our book on therapeutic massages for pets!

Chapter 15: Massage During Stressful Situations

Learn how to use therapeutic massage as a calming tool during stressful situations, such as visits to the vet or car trips.

When it comes to our beloved pets, we are always looking for their well-being and happiness at all times. However, in certain situations, it's inevitable that our furry companions will feel stress and anxiety. Whether it's a visit to the vet or a trip by car, these situations can be overwhelming for them. That's why it's important that we, as responsible owners, know how to use therapeutic massage as a calming tool to help them overcome these stressful times.

Therapeutic massage is an ancient technique that has been used in both humans and animals to promote relaxation and physical and emotional well-being. It can be especially beneficial during stressful situations, as it helps to release tension and improve blood circulation, which in turn promotes the release of endorphins, the hormones responsible for making us feel good.

Before starting to practice therapeutic massage on your pet, it is important to remember that each animal is unique and can react differently to this type of stimulation. Therefore, it is essential to observe the signs that tell us if our pet is enjoying the massage or if he prefers another form of relaxation. In addition, it is always advisable to consult a veterinarian or a massage therapist specializing in animals before performing any technique on your pet.

During a visit to the vet, for example, it is common for our pets to feel anxious because of the unfamiliar atmosphere and previous experiences that may have been unpleasant for them. This is where therapeutic massage can be a great help to calm them down and strengthen the special bond we share with them.

To get started, find a quiet, comfortable place where you can sit next to your pet. Make sure you have a relaxing atmosphere and use gentle, animal-safe essential oils if you want. Start by gently petting your pet in places where you know they like to be petted, such as their head, neck, and back. Pay attention to their body language and adjust the pressure and pace of the caresses according to their needs.

With every movement, feel connected to your pet and transmit your calming energy to them. Focus on creating peace of mind and relief through massage. You can use different techniques, such as gently massaging your muscles or using circular hand movements. Always remember to be gentle and respectful to your pet, avoiding causing pain or discomfort.

Always keep in mind that the goal is to provide your pet with a relaxing and peaceful experience, so it's important to be attentive to their reaction. If you notice that your pet is showing signs of discomfort or tension, stop the massage and find another way to help them relax. Every animal is unique, and it's your responsibility to adapt to their individual needs.

Therapeutic massage can also be beneficial during car trips, especially if your pet experiences anxiety when getting into the vehicle. Before starting the trip, take a few minutes to give your pet a relaxing massage session. This will help calm your mind and establish a state of relaxation before starting the journey.

Remember that therapeutic massage is not a magic solution for all of your pet's stress or anxiety problems, but it can be a useful technique to strengthen the bond with them and to provide them with a pleasant experience during stressful situations. In the second part of this chapter, we will discuss some advanced therapeutic massage techniques that can be used during these specific situations. Get ready to discover new ways to help your pet stay calm and relaxed! There are a variety of stressful situations in our pets' lives, and understanding how using therapeutic massage as a calming tool can make a difference in their emotional well-being. As you continue to explore advanced therapeutic massage techniques, you'll discover new ways to help your pet stay calm and relaxed during these specific situations.

During a visit to the vet, it's common for our pets to experience fear and anxiety. However, therapeutic massage can become a valuable tool to calm their fears and strengthen the special bond we share with them. As you progress through the massage session, you can incorporate additional techniques that will help to further relieve tension in your pet.

An effective technique to consider is passive stretching. This involves gently stretching your pet's muscles, helping to release any accumulated tension. Start by stretching their legs and limbs, moving them back and forth smoothly, always respecting your pet's limits. Pay attention to how he reacts, because his comfort is the most important thing.

Another useful technique during a vet visit is pressure point massage. As in humans, pets have specific points on the body that, when pressed gently, can release tension and promote relaxation. Check with your vet or massage therapist to find out the right pressure points for your pet.

During car trips, many pets experience anxiety and stress. The constant movement and ambient noises can be overwhelming, but again, therapeutic massage can be a valuable tool to help them relax. In addition to the techniques already mentioned, there are others that can be particularly useful during car trips.

A recommended technique is to use relaxing music during the massage. Soft, calming music can help distract your pet from external stimuli and create a calmer environment inside the vehicle. Choose soft, relaxing melodies that are to your liking and play them in the background while you perform the therapeutic massage. Remember to adjust the volume so that it's not too loud and doesn't cause discomfort.

Another technique you can apply while traveling by car is the use of interactive relaxation toys. These toys are designed to provide mental and physical stimulation to your pet, helping them release energy and stay focused on something positive along the way. You can place an interactive toy on your pet's seat or transport cage to help them stay entertained and relaxed.

Remember that every pet is unique and may respond differently to therapeutic massage. It's critical to observe and respect your comfort signals during the process. If at any time you notice that your pet feels uncomfortable or shows signs of tension, stop the massage and find another way to help them relax.

In short, therapeutic massage can be a powerful tool to help your pet deal with stressful situations such as visits to the vet or car trips. Advanced passive stretching techniques, pressure point massage, relaxing music and interactive relaxation toys can help to further enhance the benefits of therapeutic massage.

Remember that therapeutic massage is not a substitute for proper veterinary care, but it can be a great way to strengthen the special bond with your pet and provide a pleasant experience during challenging times. Patiently explore the techniques and adjust the massage according to your pet's individual needs. Together, you can overcome any stressful situation and strengthen your special relationship!

Chapter 16: Massages to strengthen the bond with your pet

Explore how therapeutic massage can strengthen the special bond between you and your pet, creating a deeper connection.

Massages aren't just a way to relieve stress and relax your body, they can also become a powerful tool to strengthen the emotional bond between you and your pet. While physical contact is essential to any relationship, therapeutic massages can take this contact to another level, providing a pleasant experience that goes beyond the physical aspect.

As we spend time with our pets, our lives become intertwined and a special bond is created. However, there may be times when we wonder how to strengthen that bond even more and what else we can do to strengthen that emotional connection. This is where therapeutic massages come into play.

Imagine being able to transmit all your love, care and attention through your hands. Therapeutic massages allow just that, as they involve gentle and affectionate contact that can calm your pet and create a moment of intimacy and mutual relaxation. It is a time dedicated exclusively to her, in which you can express all your love and concern.

When you massage your pet, you're stimulating their nervous system and releasing hormones that promote a sense of well-being in both them and you. In addition, massages can relieve certain muscle aches or tensions, improve blood circulation and help your pet release accumulated stress.

The practice of therapeutic massages can also have a positive impact on your pet's behavior. By sharing this time with her, you create a routine of care and attention that reinforces a sense of security and belonging. This can be especially beneficial if your pet has been through stressful or traumatic situations in the past.

In addition, therapeutic massages can help your pet develop greater confidence in you. As you gently caress her, you're sending her a clear message that you're there to care for and protect her. Over time, this can help to establish a relationship of mutual trust and to strengthen the emotional bond that unites them.

The connection created through therapeutic massages is special and unique. The non-verbal communication that is established during this intimate time can say more than a thousand words. Your pet will be able to feel your love, dedication and affection as you give yourself completely to this beautiful experience.

In the next chapter, we'll explore in detail how to perform therapeutic massages on your pet and what specific techniques you can use. We'll also discuss the additional benefits you can get by incorporating essential oils or relaxing music during your massage session.

Are you ready to go even deeper into this special connection with your pet? Join us in the second part of this chapter and discover how therapeutic massages can enrich your relationship and provide a unique experience for both you and your beloved furry companion.

Continue... In this second part of the chapter, we will continue to explore the benefits and techniques for performing therapeutic massages on your pet, further strengthening the special bond that unites them.

One of the most effective techniques for performing therapeutic massages on your pet is relaxation massage. This type of massage focuses on calming and reassuring your furry friend, releasing any accumulated tension or stress. To do this, start by gently stroking your entire body, paying special attention to areas that tend to accumulate the most tension, such as the neck, shoulders and lower back. As you massage, pay attention to the cues your pet is showing you, as some may enjoy a deeper massage, while others may prefer a softer touch.

Another popular technique is joint mobilization massage. This type of massage focuses on your pet's bones and joints, helping them to stay flexible and agile. Start by gently massaging major joints, such as hips, shoulders, and knees, using gentle circular motions. You can also gently stretch your legs and move your joints in different directions. This will help maintain mobility and prevent potential joint problems in the future.

In addition to massage techniques, you can also add additional elements that improve the experience for your pet. For example, you can use special essential oils for massages, which can have relaxing and calming properties. When choosing essential oils, be sure to use those that are safe for your pet and dilute them properly before applying them to their skin. You can also set the space up with relaxing music to create a peaceful environment conducive to the massage.

It's important to remember that every pet is unique and may have different preferences and needs. Observe your pet's responses during the massage and adapt to them. If you notice that you enjoy a certain technique or area of your body, you can dedicate more time and attention to that area. Remember that therapeutic massage is a time of connection and love, so you must be present and in tune with your pet's needs.

As you continue to practice therapeutic massages with your pet, you will notice how the emotional bonds between the two are strengthened. You'll be amazed at the deep connection you can establish through this act of care and attention. In addition, as your pet feels more relaxed and happier, you'll see their overall behavior and mood improve.

Remember that therapeutic massages are not only beneficial for your pet, but also for you. As you massage, you'll be releasing hormones that promote a sense of well-being in your own body. In addition, this time dedicated exclusively to your pet will give you a sense of connection and inner peace.

In short, therapeutic massages are a powerful tool to strengthen the special bond you have with your pet. Through them, you can transmit all your love and care, creating a unique and enriching experience for both of you. Don't hesitate to start exploring the world of therapeutic massage with your pet and enjoy all the benefits that this practice can offer. Your pet will thank you with love and loyalty!

It will continue...

Chapter 17: Massages for your pet's mental well-being

Learn how to use therapeutic massage to promote your pet's mental well-being and relaxation.

Introduction:

In our quest to care for and provide the best well-being for our pets, we often focus on making sure they receive adequate nutrition, regular exercise and medical care. However, it's important to remember that mental well-being also plays a fundamental role in the lives of our dear companions. Just like us, pets can also experience stress, anxiety, and other emotional challenges. That's why in this chapter we'll teach you how to use therapeutic massage as an effective tool to promote your mental and emotional relaxation.

Benefits of therapeutic massage:

Therapeutic massage not only relieves physical tension, but it also provides significant mental and emotional benefits for your pet. Through proper massage techniques, you can help relax your mind, reduce anxieties and stimulate feelings of general well-being. In addition, this practice will strengthen the special bond between you and your furry friend. Let's start with some useful tips!

Suitable environment:

Before starting the therapeutic massage, it is essential to create a suitable environment that favors your pet's relaxation. Make sure you choose a place that is quiet and free from distractions. You can play soft, pleasant music to create a relaxing environment. It's also essential that both you and your pet are comfortable, so you can use a soft mat or a padded blanket for your furry friend to lie down.

Massage techniques for mental well-being:

1. Gentle caresses: Start by gently stroking your pet's loin with slow, relaxing movements. Pay attention to any signs of tension or discomfort, and try to adapt the pressure and speed of your caresses to the needs of your furry friend.

2. Circular massage: Use the palm of your hands to perform circular movements on your pet's muscles. You can start at the neck and then descend down its back until you reach the base of its tail. This type of massage helps to reduce accumulated tension and improve blood circulation.

3. Paw massage: Don't forget to pay attention to your pet's paws. Perform circular movements and gently massage the pads and toes of your feet. This type of massage helps to release tension and can be especially relaxing for them.

Always remember to observe your pet's reactions and adapt the massage to their individual needs. Some pets may need more time to relax and rely on the massage, while others may react immediately. Each animal is unique, so it's essential to respect their rhythm and preferences.

Conclusion of the first part of the chapter:

We have learned the importance of mental well-being in our pets and how therapeutic massage can contribute to their relaxation and happiness. In the second part of this chapter, we'll explore additional techniques and tips for maximizing the benefits of massage. Learn how you can help your pet find mental and emotional balance through this wonderful practice. Don't miss it!

End of the first half of the chapter, waiting for the exciting content of the second part. We invite you to continue reading and discover more valuable information about therapeutic massages for your pet's mental well-being. You'll find surprising tips and additional techniques to strengthen that special bond with your furry friend. We continue with the second part of this exciting chapter, where we'll explore additional techniques and tips to maximize the benefits of massage therapy on your pet's mental well-being. Get ready to keep learning and discovering more about this wonderful practice!

Focus on areas of tension: In addition to the massage techniques, we've already covered, it's important to pay attention to your pet's specific areas of tension. Some common examples are the shoulders, jaw, and lower back. If you notice that these areas are tense or sore, you can use specialized movements to relieve the accumulated tension. For example, you can apply gentle pressure with your thumbs to your pet's shoulders, or use circular motions to their jaw. Don't hesitate to experiment and find what techniques are most effective in relieving your furry companion's tensions!

Use essential oils: Another way to enhance the benefits of therapeutic massage is to use essential oils. Some oils, such as lavender or chamomile, have relaxing properties that can help your pet achieve an even greater state of peace of mind. Remember to dilute the essential oil in a carrier oil, such as coconut oil or sweet almond oil, before applying it to your pet's skin. Do a small sensitivity test to make sure there aren't any adverse reactions.

Experiment with different movements: Although we've mentioned some specific techniques, don't be afraid to experiment with different movements and massage styles. Every pet is unique and may respond differently to different techniques. You can try more energetic or gentle massages, fast or slow movements, and see how your furry friend reacts. The key is to pay attention to your cues and adapt the massage to your individual needs.

Respect your pet's limits: It's important to remember that not all pets enjoy therapeutic massage in the same way. While some may enjoy and relax immediately, others may need more time to get used to and trust this practice. Always respect your pet's limits and don't force them to get a massage if they don't feel comfortable. Watch for signs of discomfort or stress and stop the massage if necessary.

Strengthen the bond with your pet: Not only is therapeutic massage beneficial to your pet's mental health, it will also strengthen the special bond you have with it. Take advantage of this time together to connect with your furry friend, transmitting love, affection and peace of mind. Speak in a low, comforting voice as you perform the massage, and be sure to reward your pet with treats or praise after the session. This practice will not only be beneficial for your pet, but also rewarding for you!

In conclusion, therapeutic massage is a powerful tool to promote your pet's mental well-being. Through proper and careful techniques, you can help relax her mind, reduce anxieties, and strengthen your special bond with her. Always remember to adapt the massage according to the individual needs of your furry companion and to respect their limits. Enjoy this special time together and discover how therapeutic massage can improve your quality of life!

We hope that this second part of the chapter will continue to provide you with valuable and useful information to care for and strengthen your pet's mental well-being. Read on and discover how you can implement these techniques in your furry friend's daily life. Your pet will thank you!

Chapter 18: Therapeutic Massage as a Rehabilitation Tool

Discover how therapeutic massage can complement the rehabilitation process for injuries or surgeries on your pet.

On the path to the health and well-being of our beloved pets, we sometimes encounter obstacles that require additional effort to recover. Whether it's an injury caused by intense activity, necessary surgery, or simply the natural wear and tear of time, it's essential to have tools that promote your physical and emotional well-being. This is where therapeutic massage is presented as an extremely effective option to strengthen the rehabilitation process.

Therapeutic massage, in addition to being a form of relaxation and physical contact, has proven to be a valuable tool in pet recovery. By applying specific techniques, it is possible to relieve pain, reduce inflammation and improve blood circulation in areas affected by injury or surgery. This not only speeds up recovery time, but it also helps to strengthen the special bond between pet and owner.

During the rehabilitation process, therapeutic massage can be used as a complement to other veterinary treatments, such as physical therapy and prescription medications. The combination of these tools, along with the love and care of the owners, gives pets a greater chance for a successful recovery.

One of the main advantages of therapeutic massage in this process is its ability to reduce muscle tension. When a pet is injured or undergoes surgery, muscle contractures are common around the affected area. These contractures can cause pain and limit the movement of our furry friends. Therapeutic massage helps to relax and stretch muscles, releasing accumulated tension and allowing greater mobility.

In addition to the physical benefits, therapeutic massage also has a positive impact on the emotional state of pets. During the rehabilitation process, it's normal for animals to experience stress, anxiety, or depression because of discomfort and changes in their daily routine. Therapeutic massage acts as a natural tranquilizer, releasing endorphins that promote a sense of well-being and emotional relief in our four-legged companions.

It is important to mention that in order to carry out therapeutic massage effectively and safely, it is essential to seek the help of a specialized professional. A veterinary therapeutic masseuse has the knowledge and experience necessary to adapt massage techniques to the specific needs of each pet, considering their state of health, the severity of the injury or surgery and any other particularity that may influence the rehabilitation process.

In short, therapeutic massage is positioned as a valuable tool in the rehabilitation process of our pets. Its ability to relieve pain, reduce inflammation and improve blood circulation, together with its positive effect on the emotional state of animals, make it an ideal complement to other veterinary treatments. Provided with proper care and professional supervision, therapeutic massage will strengthen the special bond we share with our beloved pets and contribute to their speedy recovery.

Continued... Once we have understood the benefits of therapeutic massage in the rehabilitation of our pets, it is important to know the specific techniques that can be used to address different types of injuries or surgeries. Next, we'll explore some of these techniques and how they can be applied in the rehabilitation process.

One of the most common techniques is deep tissue massage. This type of massage focuses on the innermost layers of muscles and tissues, relieving tension and promoting blood circulation. For pets that have suffered muscle injuries, such as pulls or sprains, deep tissue massage can be especially beneficial. It is recommended to start the massage gently, applying pressure gradually to avoid causing additional discomfort. Over time, as the pet recovers, the intensity of the massage can be increased to achieve better rehabilitation.

Another useful technique is stretching massage, which focuses on stretching muscles and improving flexibility. This type of massage is especially beneficial for pets that have undergone orthopedic surgeries or have undergone prolonged immobilization. By gently stretching the affected muscles, recovery and the recovery of range of motion are promoted. It is important to note that stretching massage should be performed carefully and under the supervision of a trained professional to avoid any type of additional injury.

In addition to these techniques, therapeutic massage can also include the application of heat or cold to specific areas. Heat helps to relax muscles and increase blood circulation, while cold reduces inflammation and relieves pain. The choice between heat and cold depends on the type of injury or surgery the pet has experienced, as well as the specific recommendations of the veterinarian. It is important to follow these recommendations and not to apply heat or cold indiscriminately, as it can have negative effects on the pet's recovery.

In addition to the specific techniques, it is essential to consider some additional tips to ensure an effective and safe therapeutic massage. First of all, it is important to establish a calm and comfortable environment for the pet, eliminating any distractions or sources of stress. This will help the pet to relax and feel more receptive to the massage. In addition, it is recommended to perform the massage at a time when the pet is calm and relaxed, such as after a walk or a physical therapy session.

It is also essential to be attentive to the signals that our pet gives us during the massage. If the pet shows discomfort, pain, or rejection, it's important to stop the massage and seek professional guidance. Each pet is unique and may have different needs and preferences, so it is essential to adapt the massage to their individual characteristics.

In conclusion, therapeutic massage is a valuable tool in the rehabilitation process of our pets. With specific techniques, such as deep tissue massage and stretching massage, we can relieve pain, improve blood circulation and promote recovery from injuries or surgeries. Provided with due care, and under the supervision of a specialized professional, therapeutic massage will strengthen the special bond we share with our beloved pets and contribute to their speedy recovery. Remember that your pet's well-being is a top priority, and therapeutic massage can be a key tool on their path to health and happiness.

Chapter 19: Personalized Massages for Specific Needs

Learn how to adapt therapeutic massage to your pet's specific needs, such as allergies, arthritis, or other health problems.

When it comes to providing well-being to our beloved pets, therapeutic massages have become an invaluable tool. Not only do these techniques help to strengthen the special bond we share with our furry friends, but they can also be adapted to the individual needs of each pet.

It's important to keep in mind that every animal is unique, as are their needs. Some may suffer from allergies that cause skin irritation, others may suffer from arthritis or health problems related to their joints. Regardless of the situation, therapeutic massage can be adapted in a personalized way to meet the specific needs of each pet.

When faced with cases of allergies, it is essential to exercise caution and to know the pet's restrictions. Before starting any massage session, make sure that there is no product to which the animal is allergic. Use organic essential oils, free of additives and perfumes that can trigger an allergic reaction. In addition, perform a test on a small area of the skin to verify that the pet does not have any adverse reactions.

During the massage, pay special attention to problem areas of the skin. Use gentle, circular techniques, applying moderate pressure. This will help relieve irritation and promote a sense of calm and well-being in your pet. Always remember to follow the instructions of a specialized veterinarian to provide the best possible care.

In the case of pets suffering from arthritis, therapeutic massage can be a great ally in their treatment. Start by gently warming up your joints using slow, gentle movements. Then, using circular movements, apply light pressure to the affected areas. This will help relieve stiffness and pain, improving your pet's mobility.

It's essential that you keep an eye on your furry companion's reactions during the massage. Some pets may feel greater sensitivity in certain areas and will require more gentle pressure. Watch their body language, as it will tell you if you're applying the right amount of pressure or need to adjust it. It's important that the massage doesn't cause pain, but rather that it's a relaxing and comforting experience for your pet.

In addition to allergies and arthritis, there are other specific health needs that may require adaptations in therapeutic massage. Every pet is unique and can have different problems, such as respiratory problems, muscle aches, or even digestive problems. In all these cases, it will be crucial to consult with a veterinarian before performing any type of massage, to ensure that we are applying the correct and safe techniques.

In short, therapeutic massages are a powerful tool to strengthen the bond with our pets. Through personalized adaptation, we can provide them with relief and well-being, even in specific health situations. Don't hesitate to consult a specialized veterinarian and learn more about how to adapt the massage to the individual needs of your furry companion. Together, we can improve their quality of life and strengthen that special bond that unites us!

In the second half of this chapter, I'll continue to share tips and recommendations for tailoring therapeutic massages to your pet's specific needs. Remember that every animal is unique and, by knowing their individual needs, we can provide them with personalized care that promotes their well-being and strengthens our special bond.

In cases of respiratory problems, such as asthma or bronchitis, it's important to be careful when massaging your pet's chest and back. Excessive pressure or sudden movements may make it difficult for you to breathe. Instead, use gentle, relaxing techniques, such as gentle patting and gentle rubbing along these areas. This will help relieve congestion and promote relaxation in your pet, making it easier for them to breathe.

If your pet is suffering from muscle aches or tension, therapeutic massage can be a great way to help ease their discomfort. Start by gently warming up your muscles in circular motions and then, using your fingers or the palms of your hands, apply moderate pressure to specific points of tension. As you massage, pay attention to your pet's cues and adjust the pressure as needed. The goal is to help relax your muscles and ease any discomfort.

In the case of digestive problems, we must remember that therapeutic massage is not a medical solution, but it can complement other forms of treatment. Before performing any massage in the area of the stomach or intestines, it is important to consult with a veterinarian to ensure that there are no underlying medical conditions that could worsen with the massage. If approved by your vet, use gentle, circular clockwise movements in the area of your pet's abdomen. This can help boost digestion and ease the discomfort associated with mild digestive problems.

Always remember to pay attention to your pet's reactions during the massage. If you notice any unusual behavior, signs of discomfort or discomfort, stop the massage immediately and see a veterinarian. Your pet's well-being and safety should always come first.

At the end of any therapeutic massage session, take a few moments to interact and soothe your pet. You can gently caress her and talk to her in a low, calm voice. This will help to affirm the emotional bonds between you and allow your pet to feel loved and cared for.

In short, tailoring therapeutic massages to your pet's specific needs is a wonderful way to provide relief and well-being. Remember that each animal is unique and that it is important to consider their individual needs when performing a massage. Consult a specialized veterinarian before starting, and be sure to follow expert recommendations to ensure your pet's safety. Through personalized adaptation, we can improve the quality of life of our beloved pets and strengthen the special bond we share with them. Don't hesitate to explore the fascinating world of therapeutic massages for pets and discover the benefits they can bring to your beloved furry companion!

Chapter 20: Continuing the Practice of Therapeutic Massage for the Long Term

Learn how to maintain a continuous practice of therapeutic massage while caring for your pet to enjoy its long-term benefits.

Therapeutic massage has proven to be an effective tool for the well-being of our beloved pets. As we've explored in previous chapters, this technique promotes relaxation, relieves stress, and provides relief from many health problems. If you've started implementing massage therapy into your pet's care routine, congratulations! You are on the right path to further strengthen that special bond you have with her.

However, it's important to remember that therapeutic massage isn't a quick and one-time solution. To get the most out of this practice, it's essential to maintain a continuous practice in caring for your pet. Only then can you enjoy its benefits in the long term. Here are some suggestions for achieving this:

1. Establish a routine: As with any other form of care, therapeutic massage requires consistency. Establish a regular schedule to dedicate time exclusively to massaging your pet. It can be once a day, every other day, or even once a week, depending on the needs of your furry companion. By having an established routine, your pet will get used to the benefits of the massage and will enjoy it even more.

2. Create a relaxing environment: The environment in which the therapeutic massage is performed is just as important as the technique

itself. Make sure the place is free from distractions and unnecessary noise. You can use soft music or natural sounds to create a relaxing environment. Also, keep in mind that the place should be at a comfortable temperature to prevent your pet from feeling uncomfortable during the massage session.

3. Adapt the massage to your pet's changing needs: Animals, like people, go through different stages in their lives. It's important to adapt massage therapy as your pet ages or faces specific health challenges. Consult a veterinarian or a massage therapist specializing in pets for guidance on how to adapt your practice to the changing needs of your furry friend.

4. Watch and listen to your pet: Every animal is unique and has its individual preferences and needs. During the practice of therapeutic massage, observe your pet's reactions and be receptive to their cues. If you experience discomfort, pain, or stress, stop the session and see a professional. Remember, therapeutic massage should be a pleasant and beneficial experience for your pet, not a source of discomfort.

5. Keep open communication with your pet: Surprising as it may seem, our pets can communicate with us in different ways. During the therapeutic massage, keep open communication with your furry friend through body language and eye contact. Establishing a connection and a quiet dialogue will further strengthen that special bond between you and your pet.

These are just a few guidelines for maintaining a continuous practice of therapeutic massage in the care of your pet. Remember that every interaction with your furry friend is an opportunity to strengthen that special bond. Therapeutic massage not only improves your pet's physical health, but it also promotes significant emotional well-being.

In the second half of this chapter, we'll explore practical exercises to expand your knowledge and skills in massage therapy. Get ready to delve into more advanced techniques that will give your pet an even richer experience. Continue reading the next chapter to discover how you can take your massage therapy practice to the next level.

Remember, your pet's well-being and happiness are in your hands, and therapeutic massage is an invaluable tool for strengthening the special bond you share. Go ahead and enjoy this exciting journey with your furry companion! Throughout this chapter, we've explored how to maintain a continuous practice of therapeutic massage while caring for your pet to enjoy its long-term benefits. Now, it's time to delve into more advanced techniques that will provide your pet with an even richer experience.

One of the ways to take your massage therapy practice to the next level is to learn to identify and treat specific areas of tension or pain in your pet's body. Carefully watching their behavior and reactions during the massage session will help you detect any discomfort or discomfort in their body. Pay attention to changes in your pet's breathing, posture, and facial expressions, as they may indicate problem areas.

When you find a tense or painful area, take advantage of more focused exercises to release tension and ease your pet's discomfort. You can use kneading, rubbing, or deep stroking movements in these specific areas. Always remember to apply the right amount of pressure, avoiding being too gentle or too aggressive.

Another advanced technique you can explore is incorporating different accessories into your massage session. Examples include soft brushes, massage rollers, or even a heating pad. These accessories can complement the massage experience and offer different tactile stimuli to your pet. Experiment with them to discover which ones your furry companion enjoys the most.

Also, consider using special oils or lotions during your massage session. Natural, pet-safe products can improve the massage experience by providing a smooth glide and nourishing your pet's skin and coat. Be sure to choose products specifically formulated for use in animals and consult a veterinarian if you have any questions about their safety.

As you advance in your massage therapy practice, it's also important to remember the importance of taking care of yourself. Therapeutic massage can be a physically demanding activity, especially if you have a large or active pet. Make sure you maintain proper posture during the session and listen to your body. Take breaks if necessary and don't push yourself beyond your physical limits.

Finally, I encourage you to continue educating yourself and exploring new therapeutic massage techniques. A wide range of resources are available, including books, online videos and specialized courses, that can help you expand your knowledge and skills. The more you learn about therapeutic massage, the more benefits you can provide to your pet.

Remember, massage therapy isn't just about relieving physical ailments, it's about strengthening that special bond between you and your pet. Through this practice, you can create a space for connection, relaxation and shared well-being. Enjoy this exciting journey with your furry friend, trusting that you are providing him with an invaluable experience and improving his quality of life.

In conclusion, the continuous practice of therapeutic massage in the care of your pet is key to enjoying its long-term benefits. By establishing a routine, creating a relaxing environment, adapting to your pet's changing needs, watching and listening actively, and maintaining open communication, you can strengthen the special bond you share. Explore advanced techniques, use appropriate accessories and products, and don't forget to take care of yourself. Keep going on this exciting journey and enjoy the many benefits that therapeutic massage provides to your pet!

Disclaimer

This eBook is provided for informational and educational purposes only. It is not intended to be a substitute for professional advice, diagnosis, or treatment. The opinions and contents presented in this book are those of the author and should not be interpreted as advice specific to your particular situation.

While considerable effort has been made to ensure that the information provided in this eBook is accurate and useful, the author and publishers cannot guarantee the accuracy, adequacy, or completeness of any information and will not be responsible for errors, omissions, or results obtained from the use of such information.

Readers are advised to consult qualified professionals in relevant fields before making any decisions based on the content of this eBook. The use or reliance on any information contained in this book is at your own risk.

The author and publishers of this eBook specifically disclaim any liability, loss or risk, personal or otherwise, incurred as a consequence, directly or indirectly, of the use and application of any content in this eBook.

Don't miss out!

Visit the website below and you can sign up to receive emails whenever Gonzalo Estrada publishes a new book. There's no charge and no obligation.

https://books2read.com/r/B-A-OZBBB-JTGZC

BOOKS2READ

Connecting independent readers to independent writers.

Also by Gonzalo Estrada

Self Healing
Visualiza tu Éxito
Cultivando Líderes
Afirmaciones y Empoderamiento
Semillas de Cambio
Cómo convertir TikTok en una máquina de hacer dinero
Cómo hacer dinero con Pinterest
Cómo hacer un ensayo
Cómo Pedir un Aumento de Sueldo
Currículo Poderoso
Entrenamiento sin Violencia
Entrevista Laboral
Gana Dinero con X (Twitter)
Ganar Masa Muscular
Volver a Empezar; el arte de reinventarse
Analiza Resuelve Ejecuta
Aromatherapy, The natural path to your pet´s well being
Holistic Feeding
The ABC of Educating Your Pet
The Art of Cosmic Connection
The Art of Feng Shui applied to your Pets
Therapeutic Massages for Pets